Why the Tithe?

by
Dr. Edward L. Haygood

HARRISON HOUSE

Unless otherwise indicated, all Scripture quotations are taken from the *King James Version* of the Bible.

13 12 11 10   37 36 35 34

Why the Tithe?
ISBN 13: 978-0-89274-128-1
ISBN 10: 0-89274-128-7
Copyright © 1979 by Edward L. Haygood
Agape Christian Fellowship
12700 S. Main St.
Los Angeles, CA 90061

Published by Harrison House, Inc.

CHAPTER 1

WHY MELCHISEDEC?

Outside the epistle of Paul to the Hebrews, there are a total of four verses (Genesis 14:18-20; Psalm 110:4) in the rest of the Bible which speak of Melchisedec. Otherwise, all we know about him is found in Hebrews.

He was mentioned first in Hebrews in the fifth chapter in verse 10. Christ was called of God a high priest after the order (rank, arrangement, position) of Melchisedec.

Then Christ is said to be made a high priest forever, after the order of Melchisedec. (Hebrews 6:10.)

Hebrews 7:1-10 presents a full portrait of Melchisedec which underscores the full depth and the meaning of the book of Hebrews, because it tells us the full story of Melchisedec and the present day reasons and meaning of the tithe.

By way of introduction, notice something about Melchisedec: "King of righteousness." The name Melchisedec means *justice,* so he is the King of Righteousness and Justice. He is also King of Salem (peace).

From these titles, Melchisedec is a representative figure of an earthly king and a heavenly priest—He was made like unto the Son of God. (Hebrews 7: 2,3.) The writer of Hebrews does not say that the Son of God was made like Melchisedec. Melchisedec was made like the Son of God. *Jesus is the original and Melchisedec the copy.*

Melchisedec was made like the Son of God. This reminds us that Melchisedec is fulfilled in Jesus Christ. That which was only a fragment in Melchisedec is completely, utterly, and totally fulfilled in Jesus Christ.

This Melchisedec, King of Salem (or Jerusalem which we now know from discoveries in Egyptian records existed even in those very early ages) and Priest of the most high God, met Abraham, returning home after winning a great battle against four kings who had captured Lot his nephew, and blessed him.

There have been many speculations concerning Melchisedec's personality, but no man can lift the veil. He bursts upon us and appears in the record without parents, genealogy, beginning or end. He appears simply as one that liveth—a fit type of Him whose priest-hood and kingly state endure forever.

Abraham was returning from the military victory and Melchisedec met him and blessed him, *the great Father, the friend of God,* thus acknowledging his superior spiritual dignity.

It was customary among ancient nations to give a tenth of the spoils of war to the object of their worship. Tithes were paid to Melchisedec as the Priest of the Most High. Thus, it might be of interest to note that the word "Melchisedec" may not be the name, but a title. It will be observed that the giving of tithes for religious purposes is at least four hundred years older than the Jewish Law. (See Genesis 28:22.)

Of this Melchisedec, there is no record of any of his ancestors; no record of his parentage in the Genesis in creation. His life is like that of the Son of God—a priest forever. He continues to be a priest without interruption and without successor. He abides in the Sacred Record, a priest continually. "Without descent" means without recorded genealogy or pedigree. (The Greek word for descent is genaloge-omai meaning recorded pedigree.)

He had a father, mother, birth, and death; but these were not recorded so that Melchisedec could be a type of Christ who is an eternal being really without beginning and ending. (See Michal 5:2; Isaiah 9:6-7; John 1:1-2; Hebrews 1:8.) One might say it is an *inspired omission*. Melchisedec was made a type of Christ, so that Christ could be made a priest after his order.

That which was only a fragment in Melchisedec is completely, utterly, and totally fulfilled in Jesus Christ.

Hebrews 7:4 says, "Now consider how great this man was." The word "consider" does not mean simply "to notice someone." The word also means "to give careful, studious attention to some object." It is used in a military sense of a general reviewing an army. This is important because in Hebrews chapter five, the writer had scolded these Jewish Christians because they were so "immature."

When it comes to Melchisedec and the tithe many present day Christians are immature.

Those Jewish Christians had heard the Gospel long enough that they ought to have been teaching others, but they were still in need of learning their ABC's. These Christians, mentioned here, were not babes in Christ; but had been Christians for 20-30 years at the time of the writer's admonition.

In Hebrews 5:10 Paul mentions Melchisedec, "Of whom we have many things to say, and hard to be uttered." He had many things to say about Melchisedec, but his readers were unable to understand them.

Up to that point, Paul had been leading his readers toward spiritual maturity. He had urged them to give careful attention to their spiritual lives and to the maturing in their faith and understanding. Apparently now he believed that he had brought them along enough to launch into the deep purpose of his writing. That is why he says, "Consider him."

Once we have given our hearts to Jesus Christ and have grown in Him, we are able to look at Melchisedec, who was a pattern of our Lord.

We might ask why Paul brought Melchisedec into the picture, since he was only briefly a participant in the biblical revelation of the life of Abraham.

The answer is simple. The Jewish Christians were familiar with their traditions. One of these was that every priest had to vindicate his genealogy. His ancestry had to be verified.

Before he was accepted as priest, he had to prove he was of the tribe of Levi. In the Mosaic system, no one could serve as a priest unless he was descended from Aaron. (Ezra 2:61-62.)

Some of these Jewish Christians might be saying to themselves, Jesus Christ was of the tribe of Judah. How can He be a priest, much less an eternal priest? He belonged to the wrong family (tribe). So they began to cast doubt upon the credentials of Jesus Christ because of His genealogy.

Paul reminds them that there is precedence for this. This is not the first time a non-Levite served God as a high priest. Many years ago, Abraham went out and conquered four kings. As he was bringing back the spoils of his victory, he met Melchisedec. He was a high priest of God whose genealogy was not verified in Scripture. For all practical purposes, Melchisedec had no father or mother, no beginning or end. He is a priest forever. As such, Abraham gave tithes to Melchisedec, and Melchisedec blessed Abraham. Abraham allowed it to happen, which indicates that Abraham recognized him as a superior person even to himself. The tithes mean "the topmost," "the pick of the heap."

His Kingly Position

Melchisedec is a character in Bible history that was both king and priest. He is so identified in Hebrews 7:1-2. Jesus Christ is also king and priest. He has a royal post. He is a King.

His Priestly Position

Melchisedec is not only a king, but he is also a priest of the most high God. In addition, he "Abideth a priest continually." It is important for us to see the religious position of Melchisedec.

God never intended to have the sacrifice of animals bring forgiveness of sins. The underlying reason for the Jewish sacrificial system was that **it prepared men to understand why Christ had to die.** If we had no awareness of the need of a blood sacrifice for sins, we could never understand the sacrifice of Christ.

Before the institution of the law and the Levitical system, Melchisedec is shown to remind us of God's intent. From the very beginning, God set out to build a bridge between man and himself. I like the Latin word for priest which is "pontifex" and means "bridge builder." In Jesus Christ, a true bridge is built. It is completed. God, who once was far off, is now close at hand. Now, every man can come boldly to God. Jesus has opened the way; the bridge is built. We have no need for another to intercede on our behalf. The bridge is built and the door is open. The access to God is clear, not only for redemption but for fellowship also.

Note in Genesis 14:18-19 that when Melchisedec came to meet Abraham, he brought forth *wine* and *bread* which are symbols of the Lord's Supper, and also of God's goodness in creation. Jesus Christ left for us a memorial supper of *wine* and *bread. By* Melchisedec making provision for Abraham's refreshment, Melchisedec symbolized that ultimate sacrifice by which man's sins were forgiven and the ongoing nurture it brings to the believer.

He Is Righteous

Not only is Melchisedec the King of Righteousness or King of Justice, he is also King of Peace because of the name of his city, Salem, which means peace. One could say in reference to Melchisedec and Jesus, "My King is righteous." This truth is specific. There can be no true peace with God until there is righteousness. Many today have tried to discover peace in every conceivable way, but they can never find peace until they find it in the righteousness of God. That indicates that God demands righteousness. Once we receive His righteousness, we have access to God's peace.

This is the consistent message of the Bible. Adam and Eve separated themselves from God when they sinned. When God confronted them, He did not at first minister to their needs. No. He first called them to give an account and asked them why they had rebelled. He reminded them of their sin and then passed judgment upon them. Then God himself took the life of an innocent animal and covered the nakedness of Adam and Eve with its skin. God moved upon them to bring peace, but not until He had first brought righteousness to them. See this divine principle in Psalm 85:10, Jeremiah 23:6, II Corinthians 5:21, and Ephesians 2:14.

First righteousness, then peace. That is the principle.

God never forsakes that principle. God always deals with man the same way. God never forsakes the principle of righteousness, not even for the sake of love. He so loves us, but His love will not keep Him from demanding righteousness of us.

How can we be righteous? Repentance and reception of Christ brings the righteousness of God, then the peace WITH God and the peace OF God. Everyone in Christ's kingdom shares His righteousness. Because Jesus is righteous, we are righteous.

His Regular Possession

Many times we are told that the New Testament does not teach tithing, but that is not true. In Hebrews 7:1-10, the author points out to us that **tithing was not from the law.** There was no law that commanded Abraham to give a tithe to Melchisedec. The offering of tithes that Abraham gave to Melchisedec was an act of homage, reverence, subordination, love and faith.

The New Testament teaches tithing more significantly than the Old Testament. Of the ten verses in this passage, six speak of tithing. Here we are reminded that tithing came *before* the law and that it is to continue forever. Tithing is an act of one who responds to the object of his worship out of love, reverence, and faith. If there were ever a strong passage on stewardship, it is Hebrews 7:1-10.

When we bring our tithes to our High Priest, we are saying, "I love You. I bow my knee to You. I bow my will to You. I gladly give my life to You." The tithe is God's regular possession. We are stealing if we withhold the tithe. (See Malachi 3:8-11.)

Chapter 2

HEBREWS 7:1-10

"See how great this Melchisedec is: even Abraham, the first and most honored of all God's chosen people, gave Melchisedec a tenth (the topmost; the pick of the heap) of the spoils he took from the kings he had been fighting" (verse 4 *Living Bible*).

Melchisedec was a man even greater than Abraham, the source of the Jewish race. One so great as Abraham recognized his (Melchisedec's) superiority by paying him tithes. (This was before the Mosaic Law.)

Verse 5 (*Amplified Bible*) says, *"And it is true that those descendants of Levi who are charged with the priestly office are commanded in the Law to take tithes from the people, which means from their brethren, though these have descended from Abraham."*

This proves that even children, or seed, of Abraham were supposed to pay tithes. If they were obligated to pay tithes, so were the Gentiles, *including the Church.*

Let us now look at Galatians 3:13-14. *"Christ hath redeemed us from the curse of the law, being made a curse for us: for it is written, Cursed is every one that hangeth on a tree: That the blessing of Abraham might come on the Gentiles through Jesus Christ; that we might receive the promise of the Spirit through faith."*

Abraham, the man of faith, was blessed by the high priest of God in his day in the paying of tithes. We, as the children of faith and thereby the seed of Abraham, are also blessed in the bringing of our tithes to our present day high priest of God—Jesus Christ. (See Galatians 3:7.)

Verse 6 (*Amplified Bible*) tells us, *"But this person (Melchisedec) who has not their Levitical ancestry (no genealogies from them) received tithes from Abraham himself and blessed him who possessed the promises of God."*

This shows that the heir of the promises of God paid tithes. Here we see the priest of the most high God had orders to take tithes of Abraham, as the Levites were commanded to take tithes of all Israel. Melchisedec received tithes, not because of the law, but because of his transcendent dignity.

Verse 7 shows that the priest of the most high God is greater than the Levitical priesthood and greater than Abraham. "Melchisedec placed a blessing upon mighty Abraham, and everyone knows, a person who has the power to bless is always greater than the person he blesses" *(Living Bible)*. Though Abraham had the promises of God, Melchisedec, as the higher in spiritual dignity, blessed him.

Verse 8 presents the key. *"Furthermore, here in the Levitical priesthood tithes are received by men who are subject to death; while there in the case of Melchisedec the picture of Christ, the tithes are received by one of whom it is testified that he lives perpetually or continually" (Amplified Bible).*

If men that die receive tithes, how much more should He who lives receive them? That is, if temporary priests have received tithes, how much more should the "Eternal Priest" receive them?

As there is no record of Melchisedec's death or end of his priesthood, Melchisedec in Scripture record is an illustration of perpetuity of life, a type of Christ who is eternal. The Aaronic priests die, and the death of the high priests is a matter of record. (Numbers 20:23-29.) Their mortality was a prominent feature; but in the case of Melchisedec, he who received tithes, lived right on, as far as the record tells us. We behold him only as a living priest, typical of a priest who lives forever.

In verses 9 and 10 one might say that through Abraham, Levi, the father of the priestly tribe, who received tithes, paid tithes through Abraham. In this, Abraham was the representative tithe payer for all his seed to come.

CHAPTER 3

GOD'S BLUEPRINT FOR GIVING

In heaven, everyone is going to do things God's way. It would be wise if we would learn that we do not have to wait until we get to heaven to live and act by the principles of God. When it comes to giving, God has a plan for us. It would be wise if we would do it God's way. God knows how to make us successful. He knows how to let us get the most out of our giving.

Here in Hebrews 7:1-10 is one of the most detailed descriptions of giving in the Scriptures. It teaches three simple and beautiful things about God's design for giving. It tells us of the central place of tithing in God's plan of economy.

The Eternal Principle

Before the law, "Abraham gave a tenth part of all" to Melchisedec (Hebrews 7:2). Long before the Levites were commanded to take a tithe from the people, Abraham gave a tithe to Melchisedec. Before the Mosaic Law was instituted, God instituted tithing into the affairs of man. In fact, many years before the introduction of the law, God led Abraham to give a tithe to Melchisedec. The Levites who later were commanded to take the tithe did not have any choice in the matter; nor did the people. (Hebrews 7:5). They did it because they were commanded to do it.

Our text tells us that tithing was introduced BEFORE the law, and it has continued since the law.

"Here men that die receive tithes; but there he receiveth them, of whom it is witness that he liveth" (Hebrews 7:8).

The author of the epistle to the Hebrews, by the direction of the Holy Spirit, gave us this brief, historical sketch of tithing because the whole purpose of the Bible is to reveal to man the *grace* of God.

On eight occasions in the New Testament, the Apostle Paul calls *giving a grace.* Giving is not a law. Tithing is not a legalistic requirement for us. It is an enlargement of the grace of God in our hearts. **Tithing is the grace of giving.** Never has there been a principle of God that is operating more surely in our day of grace than the principle of tithing.

As concerning the law and the Jew, tithing was merely a starting point. Some of the time they gave a second tithe, sometimes a third; and frequently they also gave freewill offerings. The beautiful tabernacle was constructed out of freewill gifts. Tithing was the starting place.

God simply reminds us here that the principle of tithing is an *eternal principle*. It is one begun before the law; it continued during it; and it still exists today.

The question is asked, "How is the tithe given to God?"

The answer is, "Just as it has always been done—through God's people, through His agents, through His institution." In our age of grace, that institution is the Church.

Tithing is an eternal principle. It is a grace gift. If observed carefully, it is God's way of building strong, healthy, and happy people for His glory.

A Perfected Principle

The whole emphasis of the book of Hebrews is to show how Jesus Christ perfected the Mosaic system. He did not do away with the sacrificial system, He perfected it. Jesus Christ himself has become the one complete, perfect sacrifice. He is the One who once and for all eternity has made a perfect sacrifice. This sacrifice is for us now, just as it was for someone else yesterday and shall be for another in the future. We still come to God through the blood of Christ. His sacrifice is perfected forever.

The sacrifice was perfected because it was given by Christ. If we had given the sacrifice, it would not have been perfect. We would need to keep on giving sacrifices. We would need to continue going to the priest and asking for intercession as we presented our sacrifices. By giving His life and taking that finished sacrifice into the presence of God for our forgiveness, He perfected it.

How is the tithe perfected? Can Christ give the tithe for us?

No, He cannot. He has entrusted us with possessions, and we must give a tithe of what we possess.

Can we make it a once-for-all gift as He did His sin offering?

No, we cannot.

Why?

Because we do not get paid all at once. What we give back to God in the tithe now, is not sufficient for what we may make in the future.

How, then, is our tithe perfected?

It is perfected as we bring our tithes and offerings to the God of faith and love. We bring them to Him because we want and desire to please Him, honor Him, and love Him. We want Him to know that we are grateful for what He has done for us.

So now we bring our tithes, gifts, and offerings not out of law, but out of love. By so doing, the tithe is perfected in our experience.

The tithe is only a beginning. It is just a start. We can do nothing less. Today it is the point from which we can tell how serious we are about honoring God and bringing glory to Jesus Christ. If we are not willing to give a tithe, then we need not pretend that we love Him. If we are not willing to give a tithe, we need not pretend we are going to serve Him in all His commands. We need not act as if He is Lord in our lives. We need not tell people we have submitted ourselves to Him if we are not willing to come up to that bare minimum of tithing, which the Jew under the law was commanded to do.

We come under a perfected tithe, one that is given out of faith and reverence. This is a perfected principle. If we have not learned the joy of giving God's ways, we have missed one of the greatest delights, privileges, and blessings that could ever be ours.

The tithe is perfected in another way. **It is perfected now in that God gives back to us what we give to Him.** God is not a taker in any area; He is a giver in all areas. He will never allow himself to be indebted to us. That is why I so enjoy singing the chorus, "You (make it personal-I) can't beat God giving, the more I give to Him the more He gives back to me." That is why I keep on giving because this is so true.

Jesus said, *"Give, and it shall be given unto you; good measure, pressed down, and shaken together, and running over, shall men give into your bosom. For with the same measure that ye mete withal it shall be measured to you again"* (Luke 6:38).

The principle is this: If we want to receive, we must first prime the pump. If we want to receive, we must give.

Jesus told us that if a man would save his life, he will lose it; but if he will lose his life for Christ's sake, he will find it. (Mark 8:35.) This is a principle of life. It is a principle that applies spiritually, materially, and financially. If we give according to God's principle, God will give back to us. We cannot expect the blessings of God if we are withholding from Him. If we give to Him, it will be given to us.

That is the perfection of it. It is not an unusual thing. The whole physical world operates that way. If we give our time to our employer, we receive money in exchange. We give and we receive. Farmers give their toil to the earth. They put seed into the ground, cultivate it, and then receive the harvest. That is the law of seedtime and harvest.

We should learn and understand that tithing has been perfected so that as we give, we are able to receive. God takes care of His own. He will see that we have what we need, want, and desire.

We say we cannot afford to tithe, and that's dangerous.

The most dangerous thing in all the earth is to contradict one of the principles of God for our lives.

God says, "Give and it shall be given to you." He means what He says and says what

He means. Tithing is a perfected principle for today and always.

A Blessed Principle

Not only is tithing an eternal principle and a perfected principle, it is also a *blessed* one. The word "blessed" simply means, "happy, fulfilled, satisfied, peaceful, contented."

Look now how it is used in Hebrews 7:1. Melchisedec blessed Abraham. Abraham had given to the priest of God. God also blesses us when we give. He blesses us with real joy in all areas of life. God gives us blessings when we tithe, because tithing honors God. It always has and it always will.

The very giving of redemption came from the heart of One who said, "It is more blessed to give than to receive" (Acts 20: 35).

The blessed principle is: when you give, you receive.

The problem is that we have upset the whole cycle of things. God said it is more blessed to give than to receive. Many do not believe it, so they build their whole lives around the idea that it is better to receive than to give. Check up on yourself! The truth of the matter is that real blessings come when we give.

The Apostle Paul uses the Christians of Macedonia as an example of those who have learned the blessed principle that it is more blessed to give than to receive.

"Moreover, brethren, we do you to wit o f the grace of God bestowed on the churches of Macedonia" (II Corinthians 8:1).

All they did was give an offering. Yet the Bible declares that the grace of God was upon them.

They were experiencing "bad times" in a great trial of affliction as they gave. (II Corinthians 8:2.) Those things do not go together in our thinking. They gave and the grace of God was bestowed upon them. And though they were afflicted, they had an abundance of joy that abounded unto the riches of their liberality. The Macedonian believers begged for the privilege of giving. (See II Corinthians 8:3.)

Most of us do not really know whether God will keep His Word or not, because we haven't tried it or rather, acted on His Word.

We sit down and decide that we cannot afford to tithe, so we don't try it. Nevertheless, tithing works. "Try it you'll like it!"

God honors His Word. These Macedonians did not stop to figure up how much they needed for next week. They said, "Please give us a chance to make a gift." They had learned a secret. They had learned that they were cheating themselves if they did not give. They had also learned that giving is a blessed principle.

Some people say they cannot afford to tithe. The truth is that we cannot afford not to tithe. As we give, God blesses us more than we could ever imagine.

The real tragedy comes when we withhold from God. Every heartache in this earth has come because man rebelled against God. Every heartache, every sorrow, every tragedy that man has ever encountered has come from his refusal to do what God said to do. It is not surprising that so many are unhappy in their walk of faith when they have not been faithful at the point of the blessed principle of tithing.

"Why do the people of God stumble?" the question might be asked. It could be because of rebellion against God's principle—the tithe.

The Israelites were defeated at the little village of Ai as they came into the promised land. Why were they defeated after such a grand victory at Jericho? Was their army inferior? No, they had the best army. Were they defeated because they didn't send out enough men? Not at all. The men that went could have handled it.

Why were they defeated? God said, "There is a thief among you. There is someone who refused to obey Me in your midst."

So Joshua sought out Achan who said, "Indeed I have sinned against the Lord God of Israel" (Joshua 7:20). How did he sin? He sinned when he saw among the spoils a goodly Babylonian garment, 200 shekels of silver, and a wedge of gold weighing 50 shekels. Then he coveted them, took them, and hid them in the earth. Little did he know that he was digging his own grave because of his desire. As a result of his sin, Achan and his family were hidden in death in the earth.

God asserts to us that if we will do things His way, we will be blessed. If we will not do things as He has instructed us, we will only harm ourselves.

Tithing - the principle is eternal; it is perfected; and it is blessed.

The question is not how much you make or how much you owe to God. The real question is, "Have you faithfully obeyed God with what you have?" As we commit what we have to Him, we get in on the blessed side, the good side, the receiving side. As we give to God, He will return it to us. We can begin a beautiful and wonderful reciprocation with God if we just give to Him—first ourselves and then our substance.

CHAPTER 4

THE ETERNAL PRIESTHOOD OF CHRIST

Hebrews 8:1-2 can be summarized as follows: "Now the main point of what we have to say is this, Christ, whose priesthood we have just described, is our present day High Priest, and is in heaven at the place of greatest honor next to God the Father. This is the crowning truth. He ministers in the true Tabernacle in heaven, the true place of worship built by the Lord and not by human hands. Christ is the minister of the heavenly things pertaining to man's redemption, giving, and destiny."

God desires from His heart to make us successful, if we allow Him to. Be as Abraham when he met Melchisedec and recognized his superior dignity and gave him the tithe of all. Christ is in all points greater than Melchisedec and deserves our tithes.

The Beginning ....

About the Author

Edward L. Haygood, B.A., M.A., Ph.D., is the pastor of Agape Christian Fellowship serving the south bay area of Los Angeles, California.

Pastor Ed's ministry gift to the Body of Christ is expository teacher, focusing mainly on Bible truths, faith, authority and rights of the believing ones, healing, and the work of the Holy Spirit.

Ed has been used of the Lord in healings by faith, as well as gifts of healings. He has been blessed of God through the Holy Spirit to teach most dynamically the whole counsel of God. His favorite passage of Scripture is: *But without faith it is impossible to please him* (Heb. 11:6).

Write: Edward L. Haygood • Agape Christian
Fellowship
12700 S. Main Street • Los Angeles, CA 90061

Available at your local bookstore.

Harrison House

Fast. Easy. Convenient.

For the latest Harrison House product information and author news, look no further than your computer. All the details on our powerful, life-changing products are just a click away. New releases, E-mail subscriptions, Podcasts, testimonies, monthly specials—find it all in one place. Visit harrisonhouse.com today!

harrisonhouse

The Harrison House Vision

Proclaiming the truth and the power
Of the Gospel of Jesus Christ
With excellence;

Encouraging Christians to
Live victoriously,
Grow spiritually,
Know God intimately.